THE WRITER MOM JOURNAL

30 PRACTICAL WAYS TO FIND FOCUS FOR YOUR WRITING LIFE

EVERLY REED

Copyright © 2020 by Everly Reed

All rights reserved.

No part of this book or accompanying workbook may be reproduced in any form or by any electronic or mechanical means, including information storage and retrieval systems, without written permission from the author, except for the use of brief quotations in a book review.

ISBN: 978-1-7774041-1-6

CONTENTS

Untitled   v
Introduction   vii

PART I
WEEK ONE

Day One	3
Writer Mom Hack	5
Day Two	6
Extra Challenge	7
Day Three	8
Day Four	10
Writer Mom Hack	12
Day Five	13
Day Six	14
Day Seven	16
Writer Mom Hack	17

PART II
WEEK TWO

Day Eight	21
Day Nine	23
Writer-Mom Fact	24
Day Ten	25
Extra Challenge	27
Day Eleven	28
Day Twelve	30
Writer Mom Hack	32
Day Thirteen	33
Day Fourteen	35

PART III
WEEK THREE

Day Fifteen	39
Day Sixteen	41
Day Seventeen	43
Day Eighteen	45
Day Nineteen	46
Writer Mom Hack	48
Day Twenty	49
Day Twenty-One	51

PART IV
WEEK FOUR

Day Twenty-Two	55
Day Twenty-Three	57
Day Twenty-Four	59
Day Twenty-Five	60
Day Twenty-Six	62
Writer-Mom Hack	64
Day Twenty-Seven	65
Writer-Mom Hack	66

PART V
WEEK FIVE

Day Twenty-Eight	69
Day Twenty-Nine	71
Day Thirty	72
Learn More	74
About the Author	76

By Everly Reed
BA Psych & Writer Mom

Introduction

Welcome to the Writer Mom Journal

Hey there, Writer Mom! I see you over there juggling it all—kids, partners, work, and the never-ending pile of laundry—all while trying to carve out a sliver of writing time. At times it feels nearly impossible, like one more guilt-inducing task to add to the list, yet it's a sanity-saving endeavor you can't shake. I hear you, loud and clear.

I won't claim to know all the barriers to writing you face but I've travelled this writer-mom road long enough to have learned a thing or two. I've been a writer and mom of a newborn, one-hand typing into my phone while nursing a baby. I've been a writer and mom of toddlers, sitting on their bedroom floor with my laptop balanced on my knees, writing while they nap. I've been a writer and mom with three kids under four, wondering if I'll ever accomplish anything that doesn't revolve around playdates or meal planning. I've been a writer and mom transitioning back to full time employment, learning to use a dictation app because my commute home from work was the only time I had to write. I may not have walked your path but

Introduction

I've shared the struggle of the writer mom—how to find time, how to find balance, and how to find a way to take care of myself while taking care of everyone else.

The Writer Mom Journal gives you the tools to shape your writing goals. Each day contains information and a short exercise or challenge rooted in research that will help you make the most of your writing time. Not all thirty challenges will apply to where you are on your current writing journey, but by the end of the month you'll have a pocket full of tools that meet you where you are and a few others to pull out down the road. This journal also comes with the support of the Writer Moms Inc. community, a group of over one thousand writer moms with their own journeys and tools to share, a group formed on the principle of championing one another and encouraging success for all moms with a dream.

The Writer Mom Journal is meant to be used with the free, accompanying workbook. You can download your copy from
www.writermomsinc.com/wp-content/uploads/2020/09/The-Writer-Mom-Journal-WB.pdf

Day One
Creating a Realistic Writing Schedule

Welcome to Day One, friend! The path that has brought you to this point of your writing journey will be varied and uniquely yours, but you wouldn't be here without a drive to create and a determination to share your story. Those things are essential but having the desire to write doesn't get you far if you don't have the time or energy! As writer moms, finding this time can come with extra challenges, and the standard advice of sitting down to write every day sometimes doesn't work for moms who are juggling kids, work, supper, carpooling, and the never-ending laundry pile. Day One is all about figuring out how to create an intentional and realistic writing schedule where you can allow yourself to write without sacrificing your sanity!

Your Challenge:
In your Writer Mom Journal workbook, outline pockets of time you could use for writing. Make note of what your average, everyday schedule is like and find those times throughout the day you might be able to carve out some writing time. Maybe it's at night when the kids go to bed. Maybe it's during soccer

practice. If you have younger children, do you have time to steal when they're napping? Can you get up an hour early without turning into a mombie for the rest of the day? There's no perfect equation for writing success, just do what's realistic and be intentional about it, allowing for flexibility when necessary and building in non-writing days too. Now write it down! Use a sticky note, write it on your calendar, schedule it in your phone —wherever will be most visible. Not only will it be a visual reminder of your newly created writing schedule, research has also shown that the act of writing something down activates parts of the brain associated with learning and memory. Finally, make the commitment to begin utilizing your new schedule now— TODAY! We'll check in on how this is working for you on Day Five.

Writer Mom Hack

Typing things into a phone or laptop results in "shallower processing" then if you write something by hand. So, even if your go-to time management or scheduling tool is digital, take a minute to write it on paper to help your brain fully absorb and recall the information.

Day Two
Realistic Expectations

With your schedule in place, now is a great time to talk expectations. No one needs one more thing to feel guilty about, least of all an arbitrary expectation you placed on yourself. Even so, it's still valuable to have something to strive for. So, how much can you *really* get done in the time you have? Can you write 200 words per nap-time? 500 words after the kids go to bed? 1000? Keep in mind it's better to set a lower, more achievable goal and nail it than to set a challenging goal only to be disappointed when you miss it. Luckily, I have a tool to help with that.

YOUR CHALLENGE:

Use previous experience and the table in your workbook to brainstorm your best case and worst case scenarios when it comes to what's achievable during your allotted writing time(s). From there, determine what the most likely outcome is. All three outcomes can (and likely will!) happen; but determining what is the most probable outcome will help align your expectations and serve as a reminder to celebrate a best-case-day and not take a worst-case-day too hard.

Extra Challenge

Practice keeping up with this routine for the next 28 days! Research says it takes 66 days to form a new habit, so by the end of this challenge you'll be well on your way!

Day Three
Short Term Goals

Having a writing schedule and realistic expectations is a great start, but to build on that momentum we need goals. First up are short term goals—detailed, narrow intentions specific to the project you're working on. For the purposes of the challenge, we'll define *short term* as the next 28 days. There's way more brain science that goes into goal setting than we have time to discuss here, but the short story is that the brain doesn't differentiate between what you've achieved and what you want to achieve, so if you map out a goal the brain is already releasing dopamine (a neurochemical that boosts mood, motivation, and attention) and giving you a mental high five. Goal planning is so much more fun when your brain is cheering you on!

Your Challenge:
Follow these four steps for goal setting success:

1. Figure out your short term goals, specific to what you'd like to accomplish by the end of this 30 day challenge.

2. Write them down! (See Day One note.)
3. Make sure they're specific and include a deadline, word count, time frame, etc.
4. Under each goal, write a three-step plan on how you will achieve it.

Day Four
Long Term Goals

Similar to yesterday's challenge, today we're talking goals again; but, this time, let's target your broad, overarching goals and writing vision. Treating your writing like a business, complete with a vision and plan for future growth, is fundamental and will guide how you allocate your time and energy. Regardless of whether you plan to indie publish or seek the traditional route, it's easy to feel stretched thin when so much of a writing career exists outside of the actual writing part. Being focused and intentional about where you'd like to spend the limited time you sourced in days one and two will help your feel less overwhelmed.

YOUR CHALLENGE:

In your workbook, jot down your hopes for your writing career. Don't be afraid to dream! From there, be more specific. Outline where you'd like to be in one year and in five years. If that seems overwhelming, choose the project you're working now and outline some long term goals for where you'd like to be with it in a year. Once you have those, brainstorm habits or steps you can take now to work towards those goals.

Writer Mom Hack

Research has shown that an ability to stick to goals benefits from two additional steps—holding yourself accountable and revisiting your goals throughout the term you've set. So, keep that dopamine flowing by enlisting a goal buddy to check in with regularly and make a plan to review and reevaluate your goals quarterly.

Day Five
Staying On Track

A plan is always perfect in your head (or on paper), isn't it? Sitting down to actually execute it is a whole other story. Today is about examining that execution and making changes for continued success. Being flexible with a plan is essential, especially when mom-life can throw a good curveball.

YOUR CHALLENGE:
You've had a few days to try out your new writing routine, so how's it going? Have you stuck with it?

- If so, that's great! How can you plan for continued success?

- If not, what's held you up and how can you fix it?

Use the tracking grid in your workbook for the remainder of the challenge to mark the days your routine worked and pay attention to the ones when it didn't, trying to identify why not and how to plan or adjust for those situations.

Day Six
Finding Motivation To Write

You've carved out a workable time to sit and write, but ... you don't feel inspired. The clock is ticking on the ten or thirty or sixty minutes you have to write, but unfortunately your muse didn't get the memo. There's nothing quite as frustrating as sitting in front of a blinking cursor while you watch your all-too-precious writing minutes slip away. You feel stuck and annoyed with yourself, and if you're working under a deadline you can be sure this ratchets up the anxiety.

Your muse might not be showing up, but you are! We writer moms can't rely on that fickle muse anyhow, so today we're going to use stream-of-consciousness writing to eliminate stress and get the creativity flowing.

YOUR CHALLENGE:
Studies show that just eight minutes of stream-of-consciousness writing can improve your performance and reduce anxiety. At the beginning of your next writing session, set a timer for eight minutes and write any and all things that come to mind. Don't censor yourself or stop to fix mistakes—just write. For

those of you who shudder at the thought of using any of your few precious writing moments for something not project-related, try this challenge in the head space of your main character. It will not only be a great exercise for developing that character's voice, but you may also learn something new about your character and story! Once your eight minutes is up, try tackling your project again.

Stream-of-consciousness writing can take some getting used to if it's not something you've done before. Use the space in your workbook to brainstorm writing prompts to help get you started.

Day Seven
Putting it Together

Forming a new habit is hard. Luckily, there's been tons of research in this area to help us out, because who needs more things to juggle and remember? Not you; that's for sure. Today is about pulling together elements from the week in a different, meaningful way and working towards making your routine and goals a habit.

YOUR CHALLENGE:

Science has shown that incorporating a new habit into an existing one is key to success, as is adding in a reward to keep the motivation up. For example, say you want to start writing in the evenings and your current routine is to put the kids to bed then make a cup of tea. You can piggyback on this already established routine by using the time it takes for your kettle to boil to boot up your computer, thereby making tea your cue for writing. The reward can range from the progress you make on your WIP to a tangible item (cookies…need I say more??)—whatever motivates you to stick to your routine! The chart in your workbook will help guide you through this strategy.

Writer Mom Hack

Studies have found that listing and testing out 3-5 cues and rewards to find the combination that works best is ideal for optimal success.

Day Eight
Build Your Writing Family

As an author, having an online platform is helpful; and it's never too early to start building. A common assumption is that there's no point building a social media presence without a book to sell, but there's so much more to it than creating a platform from which to sell a product. (In fact, using your author social media just to promote and sell is generally frowned upon). Your author platform isn't just for finding readers; it's also a link to your writing family—the like-minded writers in the same stage of writing as you, who share the same questions, who you can build relationships with. Chances are you already partake in social media and have made steps towards finding your online community, but now we want to take it a little further. Stepping out of your comfort zone can be scary, but the benefits are worth it! Posse

Your Challenge:

This week I challenge you to contribute to a social media platform of your choice regularly. The particulars are up to you. Depending on your current level and comfort, that might mean doing an Instagram TV (IGTV) video where you talk about your work in progress (WIP), or it may mean challenging yourself to post something on Twitter every day for the week or stepping up your engagement by commenting and jumping into some conversations daily. For those who are new to opening your writing life to online communities, push yourself to step up your engagement. If once a day for a week seems unreasonable for you then pick a schedule that you can commit to. The goal for this challenge is to be consistent and intentional about your platform.

Day Nine
Grow Your Writing Family

Yesterday was about engaging with an already established online community. Today is all about stepping out and trying something new! Whether it's a new platform you don't usually engage with or finding a new way to use it and interact with people, trying something new is great for expanding the group of people cheering you on, growing your knowledge, and having fun!

YOUR CHALLENGE:

Find a new online group (Twitter chat, Facebook group, etc.) to connect with today. A quick check of the @writevent account on Twitter will tell you all the writerly things happening there today. Search Facebook for writing groups in your genre. Scan through Instagram tags to see if you can find an upcoming challenge to participate in.

Already connected with a great online community you love? Check in with them! Interaction is key to creating a connection within an online community. You can use the space in your workbook to keep track of what you find.

Writer Mom Fact

The WMI community was formed after a webinar on community building, so we feel pretty strongly that wonderful connections can be made online and outside of your comfort zone!

Day Ten
Getting Personal

What's harder than putting yourself out there on social media? Doing it in person.

That said, there's a wonderful benefit to making in-person connections. While online opportunities allow you to meet lots of new friends you may not have met otherwise, sitting down to talk writing or life over a cup of coffee is a fantastic experience and a link to the writing community in your local area. When the time comes for finding a critique partner or beta reader, help with book marketing, and support and encouragement, the more people in your corner—online or in person—the more successful your writing efforts will be.

YOUR CHALLENGE:

Come up with a list of writing groups in your area. Start with your local library. Writing associations, such as the Women's Fiction Writers Association or Society of Children's Book Writers, usually have local chapters you can join. Check online for a local writers' conference to see which groups take part. Still coming up short? Consider reaching out to people in the online communities you're a part of to find out if any of them are in your area and know where to find a writing group close by. You can use the space in your workbook to keep track of groups you find.

Extra Challenge

Feeling brave? Contact one of the groups you identified to see when their next meet up is.

Day Eleven
Reining it In

All this talk about connecting with other writers is all fine and good, but does it help you finish that manuscript? Yes! There's no denying that having a group of people who understand author struggles and cheer you on is motivating and encouraging. Plus, the very practical side of connecting with people who can offer critiquing, beta reading, or marketing tips is endlessly helpful. Sometimes it can be too much of a good thing, especially when connecting gets in the way of those carefully crafted goals you came up with during Week One.

YOUR CHALLENGE:
Look back at the writing schedule you came up with on Day One and compare it to how much time you typically spend connecting about writing. Does your current writing schedule include social media time? In person critique groups? Should it?

There's no magic formula to figure out how much time a writer should dedicate to building a platform and connecting with other writers—only you can determine what's right for you. The key to creating that balance is determining how much time you need for connecting and planning that time accordingly. Let me speak from advice here. If you plan ten minutes for checking Instagram before you start writing for the evening, you'll be setting yourself up for failure on both ends. Even if you stick to your timeline, ten minutes isn't nearly enough time to meaningfully engage with people; and—let's be real—it's pretty likely you will get sucked into the social media time trap and blow through that ten minutes by a long shot! If limiting your social media time is challenging for you, maybe move it to after you've achieved your word count goal for the day or as a mini writing break part way through. If you struggle with connecting with people, especially when writing time is so precious, then set a goal to interact on one post per day and see how that works. Be flexible and try different ideas. Or, better yet, connect with writing friends and see what they do.

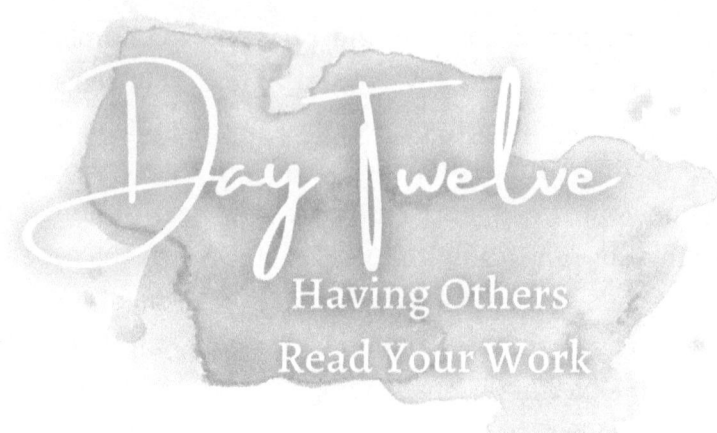

Day Twelve

Having Others Read Your Work

I see you squirming over there, and I can relate. For some, sharing writing pieces can be exciting, like a step towards publication reality. For most, it's a terrifying thought that can paralyze the ability to write freely. Putting your work out there when it's only ever been shared between you and your computer screen is overwhelming, even if the point of writing is to have readers one day! The good news is the more you share your work the easier it gets, so let's start small. Even if you're nowhere near being ready for critique partners or beta readers who will read your entire manuscript, sharing snippets of your work is a good start. Today's challenge is merely a toe-dip into the world of readers—hashtag games!

YOUR CHALLENGE:

Search up all the writerly events happening on Twitter today by looking up @writevent. Chances are good there's a hashtag game being played today, and your challenge is to get in on it. Even if you don't use a line from your current work in progress and instead make up a few hundred characters using the game's theme, you're still putting your words out there; and that's a great step forward!

You can use the space in your workbook to keep track of what you find.

Writer Mom Hack

WMI hosts an opportunity to share a line (or more) every Wednesday on our Facebook group. If Twitter's not for you, come share it with us!

Day Thirteen
Writing Organizations

We're branching out wider today and looking at genre-specific writing organizations. These organizations provide a network of writers across the globe, linked together by genre. Often, memberships to these organizations grant access to webinars, author interviews, or writing contests. Not only are there the benefits of the organization as a whole, but local chapters can serve as a critique group or help with book launches for their members. Some of the most well-known organizations include Women's Fiction Writers Association, the Society of Children's Book Writers and Illustrators, the Alliance of Independent Authors, among many others.

Your Challenge:
Search out the writing organizations in your genre—their details, benefits, and costs. Even if the cost of membership isn't something you're interested in paying at this stage of your career, it's good to know what's offered through these organizations. Some provide opportunities or resources for nonmembers too.

EVERLY REED

You can use the space in your workbook to keep track of what you find.

Day Fourteen
Family Matters

This week we've covered a plethora of different communities that can lend support and camaraderie, but we've left out one very important source of support—the people in your home! Writing is deeply personal—it's words, thoughts, and feelings pulled directly from the places we keep most hidden. Sharing that with people, even those we've chosen to be in our lives, can be tough for some. There are just as many people on the flip side—those who are happy to openly share their words, triumphs, and struggles with their people. Which side you lean towards is a matter of personality and preference, but what remains is the fact that there's value in seeking out the support within your inner circle.

YOUR CHALLENGE:

I'm not here to prescribe to you a challenge about the relationships in your life, so this challenge is more of an introspective one—a space to take the time to think about the people in your life and how you choose to bring them on your journey. It's maybe even a space to create a goal around it if you choose.

As part of today's challenge, also think about how you present your writing passion to your children. Even if you don't intentionally let them into the details of your writing career—whether because of your personal preference or because they're too young to comprehend—they're still on this journey with you. They share their mom with the craft, and it's wonderful that they do. We've spent years encouraging our children to persevere and grow, both cheering them on and being their safe space when they need to recoup. Allowing them to watch our writing struggles and successes is an opportunity to practice what we preach—that learning is lifelong, failure is okay, and dreams are worth pursuing.

Day Fifteen
The Honeymoon is Over

Welcome to the week of perseverance—a cure to the saggy middle. For anyone who's undertaken a challenge like this before, you know what I'm talking about. Week One you're pumped up and start out strong. Week Two is met with a little less enthusiasm, but you settle in and pull through. Week Three you start dropping the ball. Life is busy, and time is precious. Carving out extra moments becomes an almost impossible task. I've been there—hello every Instagram challenge I've ever started and never finished! This week we're hoping to shake you out of that pattern and keep the momentum up, because this exact problem can apply to that manuscript you're writing—you have a fantastic idea and you write with passion in the beginning, then you hit the saggy middle and momentum drops. Maybe you've hit a plot problem or maybe you're burnt out from churning out your ideas for days on end, but either way it happens. That's the writing reality we want to tackle this week because your story deserves a fantastic middle, and you deserve the motivation to make it through to the end!

. . .

YOUR CHALLENGE:

Today's challenge is to take a break! Yes, you read that right. Do something you love that has NOTHING to do with writing. Binge some Netflix, read a book, get outside with the kids, or do something all by yourself! We want you to finish this last half of the challenge strong and want you to have success with your newly created writing goals. Sometimes a break is just what you need to do that.

Today's challenge—and perhaps this whole week—might seem like a step backwards, but if you're feeling stuck and unmotivated taking a step back isn't a bad thing. Research done in the area of creativity and productivity has found that utilizing an "incubation" period greatly increases the number of creative ideas produced. This week we're going to create an incubation period by exploring new ways of writing, fostering creativity, and enriching the background of your WIP to reignite the spark.

Day Sixteen
Renew Your ~~Vows~~ Goals

Plans are great. They're a direction to head in and a goal to strive for. Plans are also in constant flux. Even knowing that, sometimes as authors we put undue pressure on ourselves to perform to a certain standard we've created. A little bit of stress is good when trying to hit a deadline or pushing through a tough spot in your manuscript. Too much stress is a creativity and confidence killer. Today we'll revisit your expectations and goals to reassess how realistic they really are.

YOUR CHALLENGE:

Today isn't so much of a challenge as a reaffirmation. Flip back to Days One, Two, Three, and Five and reflect on these questions:

1. Were your expectations truly realistic?
2. Are you struggling to achieve what you'd hoped?
3. Are you on track to your short term goals?
4. Where are you facing challenges?

5. How can you change your goals/expectations to better fit your reality?

If you're struggling, now is a wonderful time to practice that grace and flexibility we talked about earlier. Adjusting your plan doesn't mean the plan was a failure, it means that you learned something and there's room for improvement. Jot down some ideas in your workbook to increase your success and decrease your stress.

Day Seventeen
Butt-in-Chair Challenge

It's one of those controversial debates in the writing community—right up there with pantsing vs. plotting—and when you read the intro to this challenge seventeen days ago I clearly stated that the life of a writer mom is too complex to simply adhere to a prescriptive method like this one. But for today, for the sake of experimentation, let's put our arguments aside and take a look at the butt-in-chair method. I'm not talking about the way purists of this method use it—the idea of sitting at your laptop every day for longer and longer periods of time. Instead, I want you to use the idea behind the butt-in-chair method—writing whether your muse has shown up and whether you feel like it or not—to encourage progress, recapture momentum, and help identify some stolen moments to keep progressing towards your goals.

Your Challenge:

Butt. In. Chair. Okay, I said it, but that's not what I really mean. More like "mind-on-your-goals." Today I'd like you to find three-five minutes where you wouldn't normally write and get a few words down. They don't have to be for your WIP or for social media content. Heck, they don't even need to make sense or be done while in a seated position. Just grab your laptop/phone/sticky notes and write for a few minutes. This challenge may not garner any leaps and bounds for your WIP, but instead it's about practicing a skill you can build on to set yourself up for future successes. Writing during our scheduled writing times is an amazing accomplishment on its own but being able to create new opportunities where there were none before is a skill that benefits us writer moms that are trying desperately to give life to our careers. The more often you write, the more solid of a routine you develop. How much time you have to write ebbs and flows—less when baby stops napping, more when they go to school, less when you start a new job, etc. But, even when the amount of time changes, the habit of writing will stay constant. And now that we've entered the saggy middle of this challenge, maybe those handful of sentences will be the only words you get in today; but they're a step in the right direction.

Day Eighteen
The Why

This may be the most difficult and fear-inducing challenge of the month. It's a scenario I've heard dozens of writers relay time and again—the notion that people want you to tell them about your story. Sometimes it's not even something you've explored before. A spark of an idea turned into an outline, and eventually a whole fleshed out story. That process doesn't always leave time to think about why this story speaks to you and why it means enough to absorb the spare hours of your day. But, when you think about it, that *why* is a pretty important question.

YOUR CHALLENGE:

Pretend a stranger, friend, or dream agent just asked you WHY you chose to write the story you're working on. Write a few paragraphs in your workbook about why this is *your* story to write. Why are these characters special to you, and why is the message you're hoping to convey vital to get out?

Day Nineteen
The Subplot

Sometimes our stories lose that exciting feel to them. We start doubting our ability to pull off an ambitious plot or we doubt that our ideas are any good. Nothing slows momentum down faster than all that self-doubt. The good news is there's merit to every story and there was a reason you fell in love with it in the first place. (See yesterday's challenge—this is YOUR story and you've got this!) Today we're going to stay within your WIP world and try to reclaim that excitement and energy through a new character or subplot.

YOUR CHALLENGE:

Open a new document and create a short, alternate story that takes place within your story world. Some prompts to consider:

1. A prologue-type segment that gets out all the backstory leading up to the start of your WIP.
2. A what-if question that you're wanting to explore.

3. A spin-off story about a random character that makes a one-time appearance somewhere in your story.
4. How another (non-POV) character sees your main character.

Anything that gets you thinking about your characters in a new way and gets you excited. Write as much or as little as you'd like. The goal isn't to have a finished piece but to find a new spark of excitement.

Writer Mom Hack

If you're anything like me, the idea of writing anything that doesn't directly propel the WIP forward will make you cringe and you'll be tempted to skip this challenge. If so, consider the additional value this challenge holds—the piece you write today could be used later as an incentive for your newsletter, content for your website, or a promotional tool when you publish your book.

Day Twenty

The Shake Up

Writing is an inherently creative endeavor, and we writers are creative beings—we create something that feels so real and tactile in the minds of our readers, eliciting emotional reactions and conjuring images that transport them to another place. Pretty powerful gift we have, isn't it? Sometimes our creativity gets tapped out, but that doesn't mean it's gone. Sometimes it just means we need to express that creativity in another way.

YOUR CHALLENGE:

Today is for exploring your creativity and tapping into it through a different medium. Let your mind explore the world you're crafting in a different way. This can happen in many different forms. Here are a few to consider:

- sketch out a character or scene or location
- make a music playlist to capture the feel of your story
- create a visual aesthetic board or start a Pinterest board

- make a recipe inspired by a character or event in your story

Whatever you choose, let loose and let your creativity take the wheel.

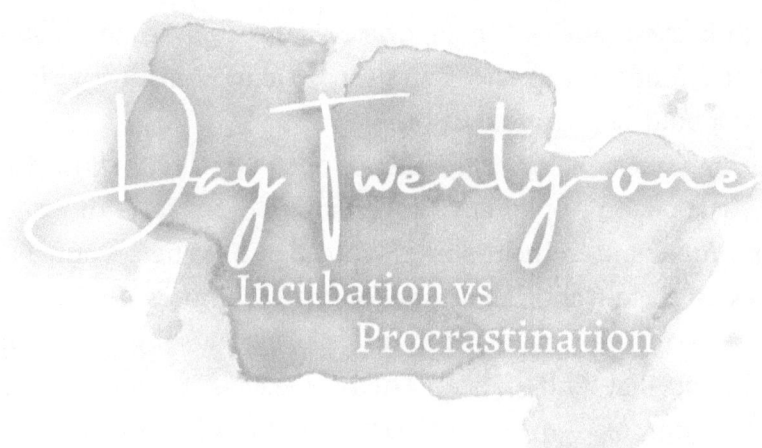

Day Twenty-one
Incubation vs Procrastination

I have bad news—there's a catch to all this incubation stuff. Taking a break to foster new creative ideas is a great way to shake things up, but all the creativity in the world won't help if you never get back to putting pen to paper or fingers to keyboard. If you want to take advantage of your creative recharge you eventually have to close Twitter, Pinterest, and Spotify and get back to that pesky plot and uncooperative characters. Research done on creative incubation is similar to that done on naps and daydreaming—all three help to boost productivity but only if you're putting the work in. Less work done before or after these little breaks means the break is less effective. Sometimes it's easy to jump back into a project after a brain-break, but other times we need a little push.

Your Challenge:

Be honest. Have you been making good use of your writing time? How many times have you sat down to write, only to end up on Instagram? Even after trying this week's tools, are you still struggling to make progress on your project? I have no research-backed advice or fancy tool for this issue, just a personal method I'd like to share for breaking out of a writing lapse or a bout of procrastination.

During your next writing session, open your WIP and...wait for it...write. Don't open anything else first, just set a timer for five minutes and punch some words out. When your five minutes is up set another timer for three minutes—a time to stand and stretch or make a cup of tea or play a song from your favourite playlist and dance. Then repeat—five minutes on, three minutes off—until you reach a point where you're too busy writing some witty banter or a beautiful description to stop for your three-minute break.

I wish it were more clever than that, but sometimes there's no substitute for struggling through a tough spot. As you rediscover your flow, the words you churn out may not be pretty; but, as Jodi Picoult said, "You can't edit a blank page."

And, if after answering the above questions, you decide your writing is at peak efficiency and this week has been a fun creative detour, then guess what? Same challenge. Sit and write and take advantage of your creative boost!

Day Twenty-two

Being Flexible

The toddler is sick. The middle schooler has a project they need help with. Your partner surprises you with a night out. As moms we're masters of many different roles, but family takes priority. That doesn't mean your book baby is going anywhere, and no one wants to be treated to a night out only to be preoccupied with thoughts of the word count goal they won't be hitting. How do we stay on track with our goals and fulfill all those other parts of our lives? It's all about flexibility.

YOUR CHALLENGE:

Think of this as a pop quiz for your time management skills. Let's create a contingency plan for all those what-ifs that throw our daily writing plans off kilter. There are endless scenarios that can crop up and trying to plan for each of them wouldn't be an effective use of our time. Instead, let's explore possible ways to flex our writing time whenever life throws us a curveball. How have you dealt with this in the past? How would you deal with these if you had a do-over? No answer is a bad one as long as it works for you—creating an alternate time to catch up, find a way to double productivity during your next writing session, or be okay with missing that writing time. All solutions are valid but having that plan in place is the step we'd like to take today. Please note that we're focusing on small disruptions that effect a day or two of writing plans. We'll leave the big, goal altering stuff for tomorrow...

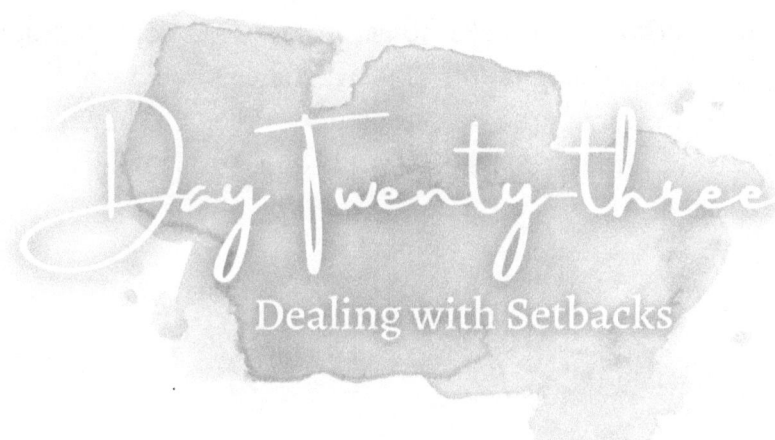

Day Twenty-three
Dealing with Setbacks

Setbacks can happen for SO many reasons. Your muse took the night off. You were a little too ambitious on the project you took on. Life. Whatever the reason, you're off track and bummed out about it. How can you get back on track? Well, maybe the question you should be asking is "What can I learn from this?" Because life is always going to happen, deadlines are going to whiz by, and projects are going to veer off track. Figuring out what to do when that happens and planning ways to get back on track is a handy tool to have on your side.

YOUR CHALLENGE:

Chances are, if you've been a writer for any length of time, this isn't a fictional scenario. Life sneaking up and railroading all your well-laid goals is almost a rite of passage for the writer-mom life. On the flip side, it also makes us masters of adaptability.

Look back at the short term goal you chose on Day Three. Imagine a life event has come up and blown your goal for this month out of the water (and maybe that's already happened!).

Use your workbook to make notes on how you could salvage your goals and get back on track. What changes could you make to prevent the same kind of detour next time? Or, how could you alter your mindset to be okay with some goals taking longer than expected?

Day Twenty-four
Dealing with Resistance

Let's get uncomfortable for a minute. There's another source of setbacks we haven't yet addressed—lack of support. As solitary as writing can be, moms can't exist in isolation. Our careers can progress within our own bubble, but it's difficult to thrive in an environment where our goals and visions aren't supported—or, in fact, are resisted. It taps into our self-doubt; and, as we discussed earlier, that's a huge creativity killer.

Your Challenge:

Whether it's from a family member, beta reader, or reviewer, writers will encounter people who aren't as excited about our goals as we are. We'll encounter people who are downright resistant to our passions. In the space below, jot down how to respond to the resisters. Jot down in your workbook who you have in your circle to rely on for support when you combat the feelings of self-doubt.

Day Twenty-five
The Messy House

Is there any better example of a setback than laundry? There isn't much I don't blame laundry for but for good reason. Laundry and all of its messy house counterparts—I'm looking at you, dirty dishes—add to our stress and are common culprits for writing-related setbacks. The messy house ranks up there with mom guilt and imposter syndrome. They all share a common thread that takes up space in your conscience but doesn't produce any outcomes. And if it isn't something that brings you closer to your goals, then it isn't something you want to spend a lot of time focusing on. The difference between the other focus-suckers and the messy house is that mess is a very visual reminder of what needs to be done. And eventually your favourite coffee or tea mug will need to be washed, so it's a necessary evil.

YOUR CHALLENGE:
I'm certainly not qualified to guide anyone through a challenge about curing a messy house. Instead I'd like you to think about what you're willing to let go of, because you can't do it

all. If you're familiar with NaNoWriMo (where writers take on the challenge of writing 50,000 words in one month), you may have heard survival stories about people giving up certain areas of life—like dishes or cooking—or shuffling responsibilities to their partner. These are great in extreme circumstances like NaNo, but maybe not sustainable for long term. However, it's a great jumping off point for today's challenge. If you want to make a push for your writing dreams to become a reality, what are you willing to give up to make them happen? What can you ask for help with? What changes can you implement to make household tasks easier and clear room for clarity of focus? Who can you delegate tasks to or ask for help from?

Day Twenty-six
Finding the Silver Lining

Sometimes a setback becomes a failure. They don't even have to do with any of the things we've talked about these past three weeks. Sometimes a story runs into plot issues too big to fix, or the great idea you had just doesn't work on paper. The project of your heart receives a rejection from your dream agent. Circumstances out of your control crop up and railroad your goals. And other times we lose our writing spark and we intentionally (or maybe not) set our work aside and focus on things that fulfill us in different ways. None of these are truly failures, though. Each step forward, every word written, every choice, enriches our creativity and builds skills in us. Seeing that, however, is the challenge.

YOUR CHALLENGE:

Can there be a silver lining when your writing goals fall through? A career in writing is almost synonymous with failure, and some would even say it's a necessary step. That's debatable, but it still stands to reason that, if you spend any length of time in this field, you'll experience the lows that come with it. What is the type of failure that would be most impactful to you? Think of that, explore it, get comfortable with it. Research indicates that, when you plan for failure, it helps your brain deal with challenges as they arise on your way to your goal. Take your greatest failure fear, reimagine it getting smaller and your future self dealing with it with humour, then set it aside. This visualization trick gives the potential for failure less weight and gives your brain a chance to process it in a safe space and in a healthier way.

Writer Mom Hack

Further research on brain science suggests that anxiety and dwelling on failure are two factors that impair performance. So this challenge is a great trick to use, but not meant as a daily activity. Visualize, plan for it, then get on with your day.

Day Twenty-seven
Tea Time

We've dealt with some uncomfortable topics this week and are going to end on a positive note. Let's dive back into our fictional worlds, because, regardless of what's happening in our lives, the life we've created on our screens and notebooks is the reason we struggle against the odds and subject ourselves to some uncomfortable realities. What better way to do that then with a beverage!

YOUR CHALLENGE:

Sit down and have tea (or something stronger) with a character. Ask them questions as if you were sitting down to have a drink with them! You can make this as casual or formal as you'd like. Write it down in your workbook or keep it in your head, but ask questions that you may not discover through your story. Coffee or tea? Dogs or cats? Showers or baths? You never know what you'll learn!

Writer Mom Hack

Just like our challenge on Day Nineteen, this activity can double as a blog post, an item for your newsletter, or a promotional tool for your book release.

Day Twenty-eight

Getting Out of Your Comfort Zone

Welcome to Bonus Week! These final three days are about taking skills we've practiced this month and running with them. First up, let's push the boundaries of our comfort zone. This entire series of challenges was built on the premise of being realistic with your time and creating attainable goals. I deeply believe those two principles are the key to building a successful writing routine and moving toward your goals, but research has also found that stability shuts down the learning center of your brain. If you're not growing, you're not learning. Reaching for things outside your comfort zone is an important part of developing your skills as a writer.

YOUR CHALLENGE:

Is there something this month that scared you just a little? A leap that was slightly uncomfortable? Asking for a little extra writing time on the weekends, investing some money into a writing organization membership, reaching out to someone you admire on social media. Now's the time to get uncomfortable.

In your workbook, write down a task or goal that's intimidating to today's version of yourself. Next, put down how achieving that goal will help your writing career. Finally, what is one step you can do today that will start moving you toward that goal?

Day Twenty-nine
Keeping the Momentum Going

We've talked about a number of strategies this month that target how to be realistic in your goals and how to deal with scenarios that can interfere with them. They are great information to have, but even better when you can incorporate them into your daily writing life and lean on them on a regular basis.

YOUR CHALLENGE:

Let's take it easy again today and take an opportunity to reassess the writing schedule you developed in the first week and refined at the half-way point. How have you fared? As you wrap up this thirty day challenge, consistent monitoring of your schedule will keep you on top of changes and give you an opportunity to put in place the flexibility strategies, in order to keep ahead of the setbacks that may impact your goals. Now is also a great time to create a schedule for these check-ins in the future. Throughout this month, we've done it every other week. Figure out how often works for you, then mark it in your planner.

Day Thirty
Mama Mantra

Congratulations, you made it to the end of this challenge! You're no longer a writer mom, you're a writing mom, armed with tools and strategies that can help you clear all the hurdles that this crazy career with kids can throw at you. I hope this challenge has helped you gain some traction on your writing goals, but even more so I hope you've had a chance to test out different techniques that you can carry forward in your writing pursuits.

YOUR CHALLENGE:

For your final challenge this month, I'd like you to create a writer mama mantra—something you can lean on when author life isn't going your way. To make it meaningful, try to think about something that stood out for you this month or something you learned about yourself, your community of support, or your writing skills that surprised you.

And remember, you're never alone in your journey. There's a whole community of women who are walking a similar path, as well as those who have come through the other side with success stories (and publishing contracts) to share. If your frustrations start to outweigh your writing joys, reach out to us. We'll gladly commiserate in your frustration, help you clear the hurdle, and cheer you on!

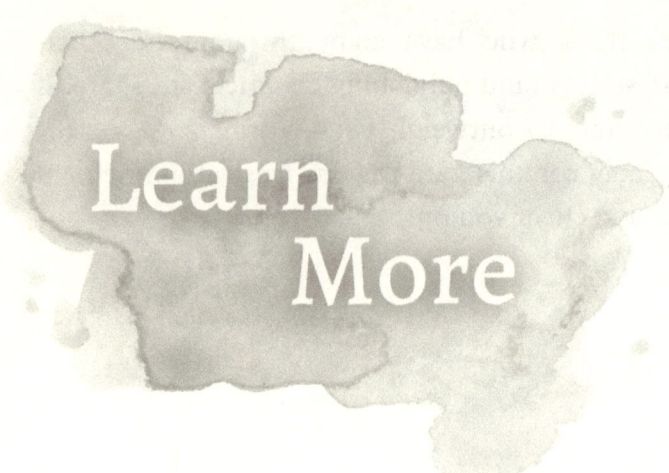

Learn More

Below you'll find the sources used in this workbook and other helpful information:

Brief Diversions Vastly Improve Focus
    https://www.sciencedaily.com/releases/2011/02/110208131529.htm

5 Science Backed Ways Taking a Break Boosts Our Productivity
    https://www.huffpost.com/entry/5-science-backed-ways-taking-a-break-boosts-our-productivity_b_8548292

How To Boost Your Creative Thinking
    https://www.sparringmind.com/creative-thinking/

Implementation Intentions and Goals Achievement: A Meta-analysis of Effects and Process
    https://www.sciencedirect.com/science/article/pii/S0065260106380021

This Is What Happens To Your Brain When You Fail (And How To Fix It)
https://www.forbes.com/sites/carolinebeaton/2016/04/07/this-is-what-happens-to-your-brain-when-you-fail-and-how-to-fix-it/#1c9c47861b81

Study Focuses On Strategies For Achieving Goals, Resolutions
https://www.dominican.edu/dominicannews/study-highlights-strategies-for-achieving-goals

Goal Setting: 5 Science Backed Steps to Setting and Achieving Your Goals
https://www.scienceofpeople.com/goal-setting/

The Power of Habit by Charles Duhigg
https://charlesduhigg.com/the-power-of-habit/
Cover Image Design: Rosalerosa/freepik

ABOUT THE AUTHOR

Everly Reed is an author of contemporary romance, and loves to use her background in psychology to create endearingly flawed characters and hard-earned happily ever afters. She's the wife of a man who knows his way around a welding rod and mother of three rowdy littles, but she's also been known to be a school counselor, chicken herder, cat wrangler, and guitar enthusiast. Everly does her best writing in her tiny office carved out the chaos of her house and within view of the wide open Alberta prairies.

www.ingramcontent.com/pod-product-compliance
Lightning Source LLC
Chambersburg PA
CBHW030915080526
44589CB00010B/310